How to Play the RECORDER

A Simple Guide to Learning and Playing

How to Play the RECORDER

A Simple Guide to Learning and Playing

Peter Lowe

p

This is a Parragon Book

This edition published in 2003

Parragon
Queen Street House
4 Queen Street
Bath BA1 1HE, UK

Copyright © Parragon 2002

Designed, produced and packaged by
Stonecastle Graphics Limited
Cover design by Red Central

Text by Peter Lowe
Illustrated by Chris Pavely
Edited by Philip de Ste. Croix

ISBN 1-40541-544-4

Printed in China

Contents

Introduction

A LITTLE BIT OF HISTORY

It's amazing to think that hundreds of years ago, when the instrument was at the height of its popularity, the best recorder players may have been as famous as rock guitarists are now. But because the recorder could not compete with some of the newer instruments that came on the scene in the 18th century, its popularity fell into decline around 1750.

Then, in 1919, an instrument maker called Arnold Dolmetsch revived production of the recorder and it soon found an eager market. Today the recorder is again a very popular instrument, and not only in schools – many professional musicians also play and teach the recorder. Lots of amateur and professional recorder groups enjoy getting together to play both traditional recorder music as well as modern compositions.

WHY THE RECORDER?

In a word – it's *simple*! Recorders don't "crash", they don't require "booting" or connecting to an expensive telephone line. There is no slot in your recorder for a disk drive and the purchase of a "scart" lead is a waste of money. All you need to do is to blow.

Because of this simplicity you can make quick progress with a recorder and yet still have the satisfaction of knowing that you are learning a real instrument with a long heritage and one on which you can perform substantial pieces of music.

THEY COME IN DIFFERENT SIZES

Recorders come in many different sizes. The most popular is the "Descant" while other common ones are called the Sopranino, Treble and the larger Tenor. You can find out about other types of recorder later in this book.

If you want to play with other people, you can use a group of recorders that are all the same size, but a group of recorders of different sizes will give you a wider range of pitch and a fuller sound.

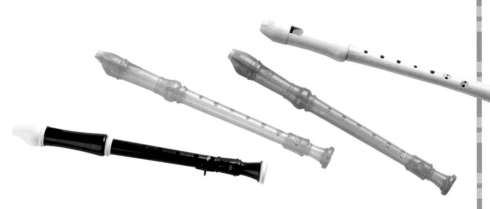

RECORDER MUSIC

When you first hear recorder music, you may think that it sounds very different from the type of music to which you normally listen. It is a far cry from rock, pop, rap or pre-programmed electronic music. But remember, different doesn't mean bad. I'm sure you can instantly pick out the good sounds in your favourite style of music. Why not learn how to do this with your recorder as you get to know a new style of music?

How to Use This Book

This book is aimed at complete beginners – adults as well as children. The recorder is great because it gives people of all ages an opportunity to start playing a musical instrument without having to invest large sums of money. To help you, I have included simple nursery-rhyme-style melodies throughout the book because they are so familiar – when playing this type of music your ears instantly tell you when you have made a mistake.

Although it is generally a good idea to seek the help of a teacher when learning a musical instrument, many of us start by trying to work it out for ourselves and we get a kick out of making progress through our own hard work. If you plan to work through this book on your own, take it slowly and carefully. Should you find any section causes you problems or contains bits that confuse you, just ask someone for help. Even if they don't play the recorder, they may be still be able to help you. It always surprises me how much some people know about music without realizing it.

Playing music really isn't that hard, it just requires regular practice. The best way to practise is "little and often". So I hope that this book will be the beginning of a whole new experience for you.

When you have learned enough tunes from this book, why not put on a little concert for your friends and family? But don't make the performance too long – leave them wanting more!

And always remember, owning an instrument is not enough, you have to play it.

Now let's have fun!

How to Assemble Your Recorder

Most recorders come in three sections:
1 The head joint which includes the mouthpiece.
2 The middle joint – this part has most of the holes in it.
3 The foot joint. This section goes on the end of the middle joint – on some instruments it is permanently attached to the middle joint.

Some recorders are supplied as one-piece instruments and cannot be taken apart.

HOW TO HOLD YOUR RECORDER

The recorder is held in front of you. Your left hand should be at the top of your instrument (nearest your mouth), and your right hand at the bottom. Please note that the positioning of the hands is the same for both right-handed and left-handed players.

Cover the first hole nearest to the mouthpiece with the first finger of your left hand. Press your left thumb over the hole on the back of the recorder.

Your right thumb should be placed under the instrument opposite the fourth hole. Look at the pictures on this page to help you.

USEFUL TIPS
- Keep your head up and your back straight when you play.
- Prop the music up at eye level.
- Hold the recorder so that the lower end is away from your body as indicated in the pictures. This will make the sound clearer and also ensure that any moisture coming from the end of the instrument will not dribble onto your feet.

Beginning to Play

Your fingers should be in the positions described on the previous page.

Place the tip of the recorder's mouthpiece between your lips. Blow gently into the instrument. You have just played the note called B.

To make the sound nice and clear, say "ta" or "tu" very gently as you blow. This is called tonguing and makes the note clear and crisp.

HOW DO YOU KNOW YOU HAVE THE RIGHT SOUND?

Blow into the recorder very gently and keep the airflow as steady as you can. If you blow too hard, you will produce a strangled sound!
The notes used in this book are shown on the fingering chart below:

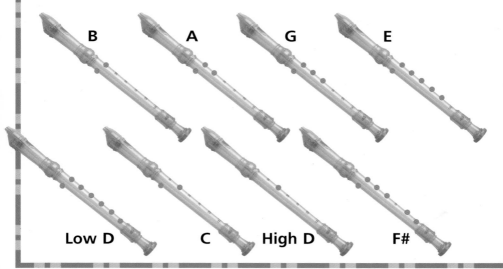

B   A   G   E

Low D   C   High D   F#

The Note B

Remember your left hand is at the top of the recorder. Only your left thumb and first finger should cover holes. Check with the picture to make sure that your fingers are in the right place on the recorder.

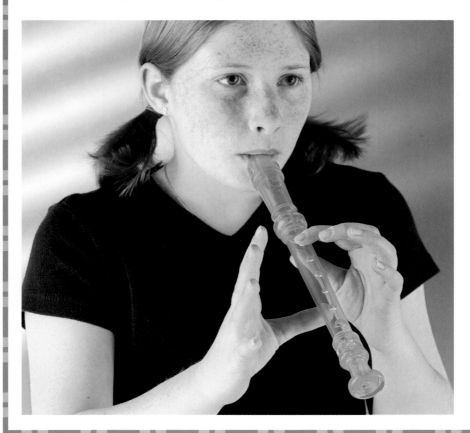

Play the note B eight times. Remember to say "tu" each time. Make each note the same length and volume.

YOUR FIRST NOTE IS B

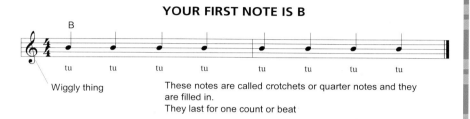

Wiggly thing

These notes are called crotchets or quarter notes and they are filled in.
They last for one count or beat

The music is written on five lines called a staff and the note B sits on the middle line.

Practise playing the exercise on this page until you can play all eight notes evenly.

You probably don't know what the wiggly thing is at the start of the music? Don't worry, I will tell you what it's called later in the book.

You can have great fun trying to draw the wiggly thing on a scrap of paper. See how well you can draw it. See how fast you can draw it. Does it still look like the wiggly thing printed on this page?

The Note A

Remember your left hand is at the top of the recorder.

Only your left thumb, first and second fingers should cover holes to play the note A. Check with the picture that your fingers are in the right place on the recorder.

Play the note A eight times. Remember to say "tu" each time. Make each note the same length and volume.

THIS NOTE IS A

These notes are called minims or half notes and they are not filled in. They last for two counts or beats

Practise the first exercise until you can play all eight notes evenly.

The second exercise uses both of the notes you have learned so far. Make sure the open notes (minims) last two counts and the filled-in notes (crotchets) last one count.

USING NOTES A and B

Open notes look like this ♩. They last for two counts or beats and are called minims or half notes.
Filled in notes look like this ♩. They last for one count or beat and are called crotchets or quarter notes.

USEFUL TIP
• Sometimes the recorder gets blocked with moisture from your mouth. To clear this blockage put your finger across the hole in the mouthpiece and blow sharply.

The Note G

Remember your left hand is at the top of the recorder.

Your left thumb, first, second and third fingers should be covering the holes to play the note G. Once again check with the picture that your fingers are in the right place.

Play the note G eight times and count the timing in your head. Remember to say "tu" for each note.

THIS IS THE NOTE G

COUNT one two three four   one two three four   one two three four   one two three four

These notes are called crotchets or quarter
notes and they last one count or beat each

Now let's put together all three notes you have learned so far in one piece
of music. Remember to count the timing in your head as you play.

NOTES G, A and B

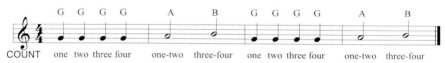

COUNT one two three four   one-two three-four   one two three four   one-two three-four

Sometimes we can use words to help with the timing of the notes.
Say the words "Hot Cross Buns" clapping as you do so, and count the
one-two-three-four section before playing this tune.

Now try singing "Hot Cross Buns" and counting the one-two-three-four
section in your mind as you play the tune.

HOT CROSS BUNS

HOT CROSS BUNS   HOT CROSS BUNS   one two three four   HOT CROSS BUNS

THINGS TO REMEMBER
- Cover the complete circles of the recorder holes with the pads of your fingers.
- Try to make up your own tunes using the B ,A, G notes learned so far.

Three Tunes Using the Notes B, A, G

These three notes only use the left hand at the top of the recorder.

As before your left thumb must cover the hole at the back of the instrument. Check that your fingers are in the right place.

"Merrily We Roll Along" starts on the note B and only moves one finger at a time. Remember to count the timing correctly by saying the count in your head.

MERRILY WE ROLL ALONG

"At Pierrot's Door" starts on the note G. Twice in the tune you have to move from note G to note B. This means moving two fingers at the same time. This movement can be hard.

The last two G notes are joined together by a line making one long note. You have to count "one-two-three-four" when playing this note.

AT PIERROT'S DOOR

French folk song

"Folk Song" starts on the note B and moves down two notes to the note G. Practise this until you can play both notes clearly.

Only the first note of each bar has a letter name printed over it. See if you can write the letter names over the other notes. Use a pencil so that you can change them if you make a mistake.

FOLK SONG

Write the letter names above the notes.

USEFUL TIPS
- Try to play each tune twice without a mistake.
- Try to play the notes B to G clearly.
- Try to play the notes G to B clearly.

Review of Notes and Timing

Review Exercise 1
We have learned three notes so far. They are B, A and G.

These three notes are placed on the five lines and four spaces which form a kind of musical grid called a staff. The lower down the staff the note is situated, the lower the pitch of the note will sound.

REVIEW EXERCISE 1

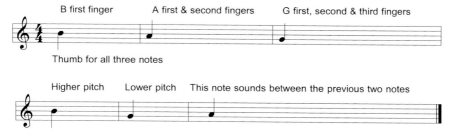

B first finger   A first & second fingers   G first, second & third fingers

Thumb for all three notes

Higher pitch   Lower pitch   This note sounds between the previous two notes

Review Exercise 2
The numbers at the beginning of the music (4 over 4) means that there are four beats to each measure or bar of music.
We have learned that notes last for different lengths of time or counting.

A crotchet or quarter note is a filled-in note and lasts for one beat or count and looks like this: ♩
A minim or half note is an open note and lasts for two beats or counts and looks like this: ♩

REVIEW EXERCISE 2

Four beats or counts per bar or measure   One measure or bar of music

one   two   three   four

Crotchets or quarter notes last one beat   Minims or half notes last two beats

one   two   three   four   one-two   three-four

Review Exercise 3

The music may have a mixture of crotchets and minims in each bar.
Provided the music has a "4 over 4" time signature at the beginning, then
the beats in each bar or measure will always add up to four counts.

Four crotchets or quarter notes = 4 beats.
Two minims or half notes = 4 beats.
Two crotchets or quarter notes and one minim or half note = 4 beats.

REVIEW EXERCISE 3

One count for each note   Two counts for each note

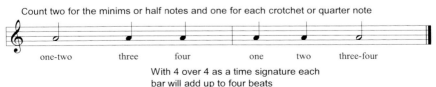

one   two   three   four   one-two   three-four

Count two for the minims or half notes and one for each crotchet or quarter note

one-two   three   four   one   two   three-four

With 4 over 4 as a time signature each
bar will add up to four beats.

More B, A, G Tunes

In these next tunes you are only given the name of the first note. Try to read the rest of the music without writing the names of the other notes on the music. Remember to count the rhythm as you play.

AU CLAIR DE LA LUNE

In the "Harvest Hymn" the minims or half notes are tied together to make long notes lasting four beats. However, look carefully at bar number four. You will notice that the two minims or quarter notes in that bar are not tied together and so they must be played as two separate notes lasting two beats each.

HARVEST HYMN

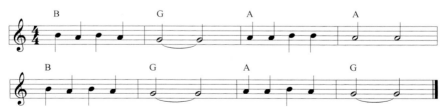

In the tune "Hopping Along" make sure that you play clear notes when going from G to B. Make this tune sound bouncy like a frog hopping.

HOPPING ALONG

Treble clef   Bar line   Double bar line

MORE ABOUT WRITTEN MUSIC

• The music is divided up into bars. The vertical lines on the staff that separate the sections of music are called bar lines.

• Each of the three tunes on this page is divided into four bars.

• At the end of each tune is a double bar line to denote the end.

• The "wiggly" sign that you tried to draw earlier on page 15 is called a treble clef. The treble clef is placed at the beginning of each staff and is also known as the G clef because it is looped around the line of G.

• Playing music to other people is great fun. When you feel ready, try out some of the tunes you have learned so far.

How to Play Really Long Notes

To play really long notes you have to stand or sit properly. I'll explain a little bit about correct posture.

Your Back

Whether you play the recorder standing or sitting, always keep your back straight. Though it's great for watching TV, relaxing in a soft comfortable chair is not a good idea when playing the recorder.

Your Head and Shoulders

Hold your head up and keep your shoulders relaxed. You should not raise your shoulders when you breathe in.

Breathing In

Make your chest feel as wide as possible. Breathe in deeply and fill the space under your waistband with air.

Your Mouth and Wrists

Your mouth and lips should be relaxed. Keep your wrists as straight as possible.

LONG NOTES

We can play long notes by tying notes together. Two minims or half notes tied together will last four beats. There is also a single note that lasts four beats all on its own. We call it a semibreve or whole note. You can see what it looks like in the example on this page.

PLAYING LONG NOTES

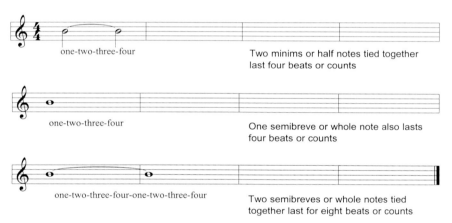

one-two-three-four

Two minims or half notes tied together last four beats or counts

one-two-three-four

One semibreve or whole note also lasts four beats or counts

one-two-three-four-one-two-three-four

Two semibreves or whole notes tied together last for eight beats or counts

HOW LONG A NOTE CAN YOU PLAY?

ENDING A NOTE

Don't just run out of blow when you come to finish a note. Instead push your tongue forward against your top teeth and the note should stop cleanly.

A New Note to Remember

To play the note E put your fingers on the recorder as if you are going to play G. Now cover the next two holes with the first two fingers of your right hand. Blow this new note very gently. The lower notes do not need as much breath as the higher ones.

NEW NOTE E and OLD NOTE G

The next tune is called "Folk Dance" and it uses all the notes you have learned so far. Play the tune slowly at first and speed up as you get used to the notes and counting.

Remember to play the open notes for two counts or beats and the filled-in notes for one count or beat. If you go wrong when playing a piece, you don't have to go right back to the beginning again. Just go back a bar or two and pick up the tune there.

FOLK DANCE

IMPORTANT THINGS TO REMEMBER
- Always play with your fingers flat.
- Always support the recorder with your right thumb.
- Blow the notes gently, especially the lower ones.
- Make sure you cover the holes properly.

Tunes Using B, A, G and the New Note E

So far all of the tunes in this book have used the time signature of "4 over 4". You have to count four crotchets or quarter notes to each bar.

On the opposite page you will see a new time signature of "2 over 4". In this new time signature you only have to count two crotchets or quarter notes to each bar.

SPRING TIME

Peter Lowe

The counting of the second line is the same as the first

"Little March" is in the new time signature "2 over 4". Remember, count two beats to each bar. You could also count Left, Right like a soldier marching.

LITTLE MARCH

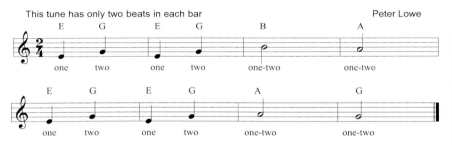

This tune has only two beats in each bar

Peter Lowe

Be very careful when playing the tune "Falling Down" that you cover the holes properly when going from the note G to E.

FALLING DOWN

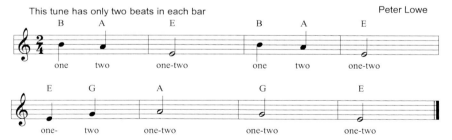

This tune has only two beats in each bar

Peter Lowe

Repeats

When we want to repeat a piece of music, there is no need to write it out all over again. You can just repeat it, and there is a special musical sign to tell you when to repeat the whole or part of a tune. You can see it in the example below.

REPEAT SIGNS

Play everything between the repeat signs again

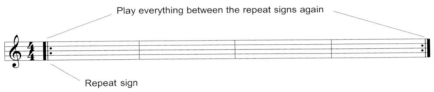

Repeat sign

Sometimes you only have to repeat a small section of a tune. Then the music looks like this.

REPEATING A SMALL SECTION OF MUSIC

Repeat sign

Play everything between
the repeat signs again

When playing "Melody One" repeat the whole tune. You will play bars 1, 2, 3, 4, 1, 2, 3, 4.

MELODY ONE
Repeat the whole tune

When playing "Melody Two" repeat only the section between the repeat signs. This means you play bars 1, 2, 3, 2, 3, 4.

MELODY TWO
Repeat only part of the tune

Play this part twice

RECAP
• Repeat the music between the "repeat signs".
• Sometimes you have to repeat the whole tune.
• Sometimes you only have to repeat a section of the tune.

The Crochet Rest

Sometimes in music there are gaps when no sound is made. In these cases, instead of a note we use a rest symbol. There are different symbols to tell you the length of each rest as the example below illustrates.

RESTS

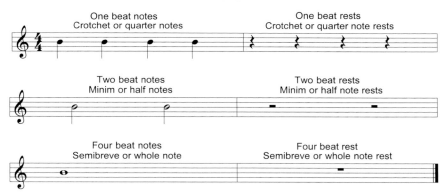

Even if there are rests in the music, each bar will still contain the same number of beats per bar as the time signature indicates at the beginning of the tune.

A tune with a time signature of "4 over 4" may have a combination of notes and rests but each bar will still add up to four beats or counts.

A TUNE WITH CROCHET OR QUARTER NOTE RESTS

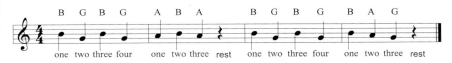

A TUNE WITH MINIM OR HALF NOTE RESTS

A TUNE WITH SEMIBREVE OR WHOLE NOTE RESTS

If a tune has a time signature of "2 over 4", the notes and rests will add up to two beats or counts per bar

CUCKOO

Peter Lowe

REMINDERS ABOUT RESTS
- The semibreve or whole note rest hangs from the line.
- The minim or half note rest sits on the line.
- The crotchet or quarter note rest crosses three lines.
- The crotchet or quarter note rest is really hard to draw (try it).

Melodies With Rests

The tunes on this page contain all the notes you have learned so far in this book. They also use the two time signatures that you have learned. All note and rest lengths have been included in these melodies.

CHINESE DANCE

Peter Lowe

LITTLE BIRD

Peter Lowe

LITTLE DANCE

Peter Lowe

B A G	rest	E G	B A G	rest	E
one two three	rest	one-two three-four	one two three	rest	one-two rest-rest

B A G	E A	G A G	E
one two three rest	one-two three-four	one two three rest	one-two-three-four

PLAY TIME

Peter Lowe

B A G E	B A G E	G A	
one two three four	one two three four	one-two three-four	rest-rest-rest-rest

B A G E	B A G A	B A	E
one two three four	one two three four	one-two three-four	one-two rest-rest

PRACTICE TIPS

• Try to read the music in your head without playing it on the recorder. Sing the tune to yourself in your head.

• Some people find it easier to clap the rhythm through before trying to play the tune.

• Look at the music and imagine the fingering of each note.

• Remember – if you can't think it, you can't play it.

A New Note, and How to Play Short Notes

To play the new note – Low D – start by playing an E. Then put the third finger of your right hand on the next hole down. Use the picture to help you with the fingering.

You will notice that the new hole you cover to make the note Low D consists of two small holes rather than one large one. Make sure that you are careful to cover both the small holes.

The Low D is written just underneath the bottom line of the staff.

LOW D

HOW TO PLAY REALLY SHORT NOTES

The notes that we have played so far have lasted for one, two or four counts or beats. But there is a shorter note called a quaver or eighth note. Quavers or eighth notes can be grouped together in twos or fours. When you count two quavers or eighth notes you say "and" for the second one.

QUAVERS OR EIGHTH NOTES

Four quavers or eighth notes groups

Two quavers or eighth notes groups

COUNT one & two & three & four &   one & two   three & four

The first version of "Chopsticks" has no quavers or eighth notes. The second version of "Chopsticks" has quavers or eighth notes in groups of two and four. Get used to playing the first arrangement before trying out the one with quavers or eighth notes.

CHOPSTICKS
Written with no quavers or eighth notes

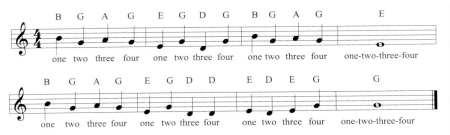

CHOPSTICKS
Written with quavers or eighth notes

Breathing

When playing the recorder, it is important to take a breath in the right place so that you don't interrupt the flow of the music. There are symbols called "breath marks" that appear in the music. They look like this ✓ and tell you when to breathe. When taking a breath, you should not remove the recorder from your mouth.

OLD MACDONALD HAD A FARM

Old Macdonald Had A Farm

When playing this tune try to sing the words in your head. When you become good at playing "Old Macdonald Had A Farm" other people may want to sing along as you play. Don't let this put you off!

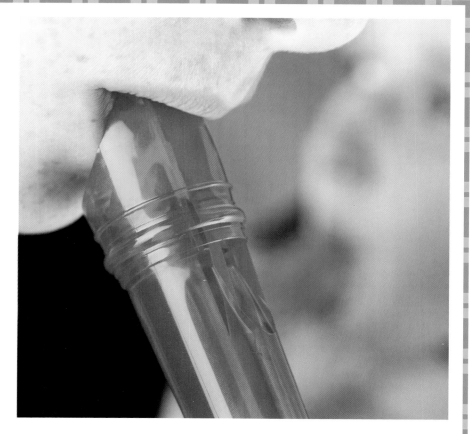

COUNTING QUAVERS OR EIGHTH NOTES

Counting these small notes can take a little time to master so don't get frustrated; just keep trying and you will get there.

The tongue movement for the "tu" sound will have to be quicker when playing these short notes.

Introducing a New Time Signature

So far in this book we have played music with either two or four counts in each bar. Our new time signature has three counts or beats in each bar. Look at the music below and you will see "3 over 4" at the beginning. This means that there is a strong beat in the music every third beat instead of every second or fourth beats.

MELODY IN 3/4

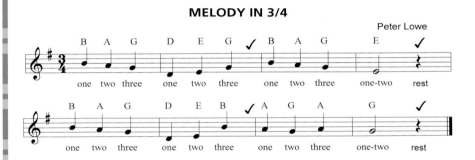

The beginning of the tune "There's A Hole In My Bucket", which is the next example, starts with a rest that lasts for two counts. Because of this rest, the first note is called an "up beat". Often this first rest is not shown on the music.

It may help to count the first two rests in your head. You will need to count "one-two" before you start playing.

THERE'S A HOLE IN MY BUCKET

G A B D D   E G D   E G ✓D E G   G A

There's a hole in my   buck- et dear   Li- sa,   dear Li- sa there's a

B D D   E G ✓ D   E   G   A   G   ✓

hole in the   buck- et,   dear   Li- sa   a   hole.

SHARP NOTES

You may have noticed that at the beginning of "There's A Hole In My Bucket" and "Old MacDonald" there is a funny symbol that looks like this ♯. It is called a sharp sign. This symbol affects the note F and by putting it at the beginning of every staff it becomes unnecessary to write ♯ each time the note F appears. This is a key signature but it does not affect the notes you are playing at the moment. I explain more about it on pages 56-57.

Dotted Notes

A dot placed after a note extends the note by half of its original value. Therefore a minim or half note with a dot after it is worth three counts or beats.

DOTTED NOTES

Remember to count three beats for each bar that has a dotted minim or half note. Count one beat for each crotchet or quarter note.

LITTLE WALTZ

The next example that I want you to play is a traditional tune called "Big Ben". Notice the repeat signs and breath marks. Your fingering will have to be accurate when playing from note A to note D.

BIG BEN

MORE THINGS TO DO
• Try to find some recordings of recorder music. When you think that you don't want to practise any more, they may give you the inspiration to keep trying.
• Recorders have been popular instruments for hundreds of years. See if you can find out for how long?

More Dotted Notes

Remember a dot after a note makes that note half as long again. So a dotted crotchet or dotted quarter note lasts for one and half beats.

In the first bar of "Example One" the crotchet or quarter note is tied to the quaver or eighth note, so you must play these as one long note.

In the second bar the tied notes are written as a dotted crotchet or quarter note. Both these bars are counted the same way. You will notice that a single quaver or eighth note has a tail. Groups of quavers or eighth notes are joined together with a horizontal bar. With a single quaver or eighth note that bar is curved and lies away from the stem of the note.

EXAMPLE 1
Dotted crochets or quarter notes

Single quaver or eighth note

one - two   &   three   four   one-two   &   three   four

If you have problems playing this timing, try the next tune, it may help.

This is the melody "Merrily We Roll Along" that you played at the beginning of this book on pages 20-21. Notice that this time I have included some dotted crotchet or quarter notes in bars number one, five and seven – these dotted notes give the melody a flowing rhythm.

46

MERRILY WE ROLL ALONG
With dotted crochets or quarter notes

The Note C

Put your fingers on the recorder as if you are going to play the note A.
Now lift your first finger off the first hole leaving your thumb and middle
finger in place.

In written music the note C is positioned in the space above the middle line of the staff. Notes above the middle or B line have their sticks pointing down. The note B can have its stick pointing either up or down. The notes below B have their sticks pointing up.

THIS IS NOTE C
Notice that the sticks point down

one two three four   one-two three-four   one two three four   one-two-three-four

Always keep your fingers ready to play other notes. "Exercise One" will help you to keep your fingers over the other holes ready to play the changing notes.

EXERCISE 1

"Exercise Two" will also help to keep your fingers in the correct place. To keep your recorder steady, support it with your right thumb.

EXERCISE 2

one two three-four   one two three-four   one two three-four   one two three-four

Staccato Notes

A dot written above or below a note means that you should play the note separately instead of running the notes together. We call this playing staccato. Playing staccato makes the note sound cut short. To make this sound we say the word "tut" instead of "tu".

EXERCISE 1

The staccato dots are not like the ones you learned previously that go behind a note to make it longer. These dots go above or below notes.

EXERCISE 2

The melody of the final example "Shave And A Haircut" has staccato marks both above and below the notes.

There is no counting advice under the notes, so you must try to work this one out yourself. Try to commit this one to memory and play it frequently – it's good practice.

SHAVE AND A HAIRCUT

The Note High D

Put your fingers on the recorder as if you are going to play the C that we have just learned. Then remove your left thumb. This is a High version of the Low D that you learned previously on pages 38-39.

High D is written on the fourth line of the staff as this example shows.

THIS IS THE NOTE HIGH D

one-two-three-four   one-two   three-four   one two three four   one-two

"Exercise One" will help you to get used to playing the High D with other notes.

EXERCISE 1

"Exercise Two" can be a little tricky so start very slowly and persevere until you get the fingering correct. Make each note in this exercise the same length.

EXERCISE 2

Slur Lines

In "Ding Dong Merrily On High" that is printed on this page you will notice a line going over the four quavers or eighth notes in the first and fifth bars. This is called a slur line. Play the notes in the slur line smoothly by only tonguing the first note of the group. In other words think of the slurred lines as brackets and only tongue at the beginning of each bracket. Slurs are the opposite of staccato notes.

DING DONG MERRILY ON HIGH

Ding dong mer-ri-ly on high, the cha-pel bells are ring - ing.

Ding dong ve-ri-ly the sky is full of an- gels sing - ing.

These tunes are becoming much harder now but don't become frustrated with them if you cannot seem to master them at first. Remember to practise a little every day and things will get easier.

In the 15th century King Henry VII of England had several recorder players in his court. They didn't get to that lofty position without realizing the need to practise, practise, practise.

The Note F#

Put your fingers on the recorder as if you are going to play the Low D. Now lift the first finger of your right hand. This note is called F sharp, or in musical notation F#.

F# sits in the bottom space on the staff just above the E line.

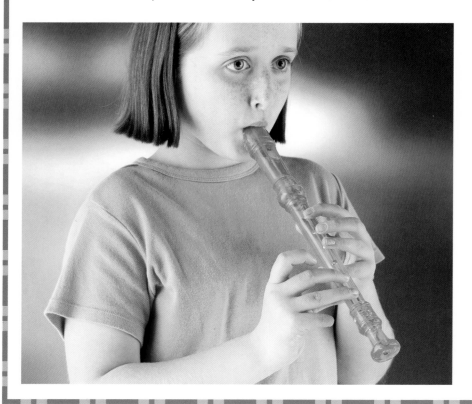

The sharp symbol comes after the note, F#. The sharp symbol (#) can be put at the beginning of the music. This is called a key signature and would mean that all the F notes in the tune are sharp.

THIS IS THE NOTE F#

"Exercise One" gets you used to fingering the new note F#. Play the note slowly at first. Notice the sharp symbol at the beginning of the music making all the F notes F#.

EXERCISE 1

"Exercise Two" has three beats in each bar. Remember that the time signature (three over four) at the start of the music gives you this information.

EXERCISE 2

The Galway Piper

The melody "The Galway Piper" uses the new notes C, High D and F# that we have just learned.

This is a fun tune to play. Start slowly and think out the fingering carefully. There are no words to help you with this tune, so you will have to work it out from the music.

THE GALWAY PIPER

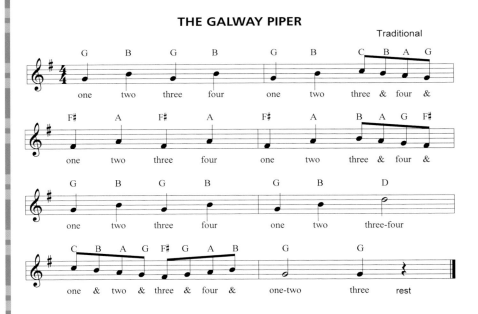

When you get good at this tune you can play it really fast. How fast can you play it?

Shortnin' Bread

At the beginning of "Shortnin' Bread" there are two sharp symbols. They apply to the notes F and C, making both these notes sharp.

Once again, by putting the sharp signs at the beginning of every staff it becomes unnecessary to write # each time the C and F appear.

SHORTNIN' BREAD

Traditional

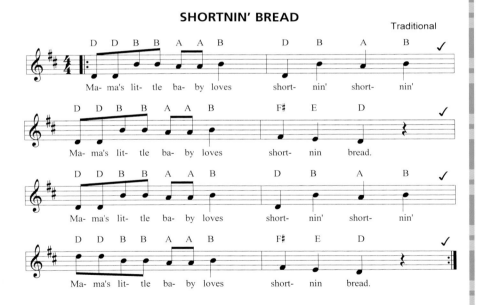

The sharp symbols form what is called a key signature. Sometimes not all the notes indicated as sharp in the key signature will appear in the melody.

Polly Wolly Doodle

Play this melody and sing the words to yourself in your head as you do so. This is a long piece of music so don't get frustrated if you can't play it all the way through without a mistake.

POLLY WOLLY DOODLE

Traditional

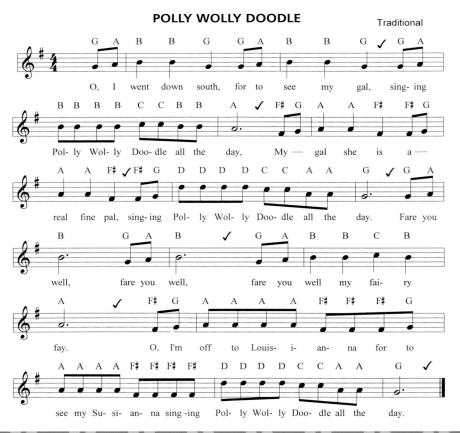

If you go wrong anywhere in the music, then just go back to the previous "breath mark" rather than the beginning of the whole melody.

You will notice that the first bar of music only has one beat written as two quavers or eighth notes. The last bar finishes with a dotted minim or half note worth three beats. The beats in the first and last bars added together make four whole counts.

OLD RECORDERS

The earliest recorder-style instrument ever found was made approximately 25,000 years ago. This first recorder was carved from bone and was fashioned in the Stone Age at a time when people lived in caves.

Today, in a world where modern gadgets go out of date almost as soon as they come on the market, it is good to think that the simple recorder has been successful and popular for such a very long time.

Some More Tunes to Play

You have learned eight notes so far and these already enable you to play many tunes. Why not visit a music shop and look for other tunes that you can play.

If you find when you have mastered all the tunes in this book that you would like to learn more notes, ask for help at your school or visit the local music shop again. Someone will be able to help you or put you in touch with somebody who can teach you more about playing the recorder.

To keep you on your toes, here are two more tunes to add to your repertoire.

YANKEE DOODLE

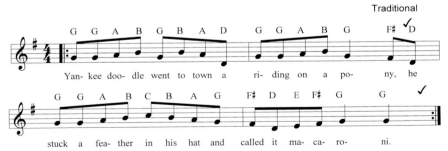

Traditional

Yan- kee doo- dle went to town a ri- ding on a po- ny, he stuck a fea- ther in his hat and called it ma- ca- ro- ni.

POP GOES THE WEASEL

A key signature with two sharps

Traditional

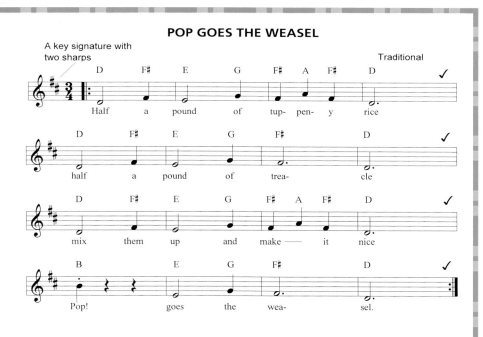

Half a pound of tup- pen- y rice

half a pound of trea- cle

mix them up and make —— it nice

Pop! goes the wea- sel.

63

Recorders Big and Small

The largest recorder is the sub-contrabass which stands over 3m (10ft) high. The smallest recorder is the tiny Garklein and this is only 12cm (4.75in) long.

Recorders are often made from wood as well as plastic, but wooden recorders can be expensive so a plastic one is a good choice for a first-time purchase.

Have fun playing your recorder and remember there are professional recorder players who make a living from playing this simple instrument. Practise hard and one day you could be one too!